Dedication

If yo

Have

Wet yo ... tears because of thought intrusio

Are in the faith community, yet struggle with reaching out for help

Are seeking answers for thought intrusions

Want to understand the battle of the mind

Are managing your mind day by day.

Then this book is dedicated to you

Acknowledgements

My amazing, caring, super focused, Jesus-loving husband, Jonathan. Thanks for being my partner and doing life with me.

My children, Samuel and Hanita, have been stealthily used by the Lord to help me manage my mind battles. I love you so much.

My wonderful mother from whom I inherited much of my mental wiring, and my amazing family. Thanks for being such an encouragement to me.

I am grateful for my church family, City Chapel, one of the platforms where I honed my notes on the mind.

The journey of labelling my mind battles started with Women's World and the myriad of speaking engagements. Thanks to every client, friend, and mentee who has been through my practice and can attest to emotional and mental changes. You have made this journey bearable and worthwhile.

I give thanks to God for the influence of my mentors, teachers, and Christian forebears in the writing of this book.

A special thanks to Mrs Toyin Onabowu of The Heritage Publishers for her tireless professionalism and joyful demeanour in editing and publishing this book.

Andy Colthart, my ever faithful and available graphic designer for the book cover.

My dear friend Jayne Banful, my first ever informal counsellor. You made me enjoy finding out more about the battle of the mind, and in our meeting up for lunch, travelling and just chilling, your dedication to being a therapist effortlessly rubbed off on me.

Dr Akindotun Merino, thanks for challenging me to become a certified practitioner and for being my supervisor. My journey to Christianity started with you and today you are still a pillar in my life.

Contents

Introduction

The Battle of the Mind is a phenomenon common to every gender, class, religion, creed, and culture. It is no respecter of persons, and people worldwide tend to grapple with the same issues.

As a Christian leader, I have been privileged to walk alongside the rich, poor, illiterate, literate, middle, upper and lower class, and can categorically state that mind matters do not discriminate. Being a Christian does not exclude you and me from the battle of our minds. If it did, there would be no divorces in the Church, and

Christians wouldn't have mental breakdowns. Young and old must deal with it.

Knowing I was not alone in dealing with this was quite soothing to me. So, after years of ignorance, self-assessments, reading lots of materials on the mind, undergoing training, helping people, and learning day by day to win this battle, I decided to share my story and the techniques employed to overcome this area of my life.

I had often wondered whether constantly having to rein my mind in would be with me forever and eventually had to radically accept that fact: it will. This acceptance resulted from self-education, undertaking several mind certification programs, which included CBT, Informed Trauma Care, Advanced Trauma Care Certification, setting up my coaching practice, and supervision with a

Behavioural Psychology Professor who has been at it for more than two decades.

With research, self-study, and continuous reflection on the way my mind thinks, I came to understand my triggers and can now deal with them appropriately. The journey to mastering my mind is also why I set up the Mind and Purpose Program - a one to one/group self-help initiative - to equip with the relevant resources, my clients and anyone who signs up for the workshop or reaches out to me.

The tools and tips I have applied for more than twenty years have proved that the battle is winnable. One thing is needed – consistently practising and using the right tools to bring the mind to a place of calmness and peace.

Having experienced the challenges resulting from a mind that seems to be out of control or is bombarded with random, repetitive, and sometimes even toxic thoughts, I am passionate about helping you overcome mind issues and thought processes that hinder you from being your true self. Rest assured that I have successfully overcome the issues every time.

The way each of us will approach the constant mind wrestling bout will be different. However, the tips and tools are generally the same. This book seeks to explain, in practical, relatable, and straightforward terms, the process by which I have kept and still keep my mind in constant check.

Foreword

"It has taken a lot of personal commitment to reach the place where my thoughts and my heart's wicked imaginations do not control my actions, even if the thoughts and negative imaginations are overwhelming."
-Pastor Abbiih Oloyede

I have been friends with Abbiih for over three decades and can testify to her struggles and healing from obsessive thoughts. She is also a graduate of Jars Institute Trauma Care Program, which makes me doubly proud to write this foreword.

Oh, My Mind! is an amazing addition to the trauma healing literature. The book is written from a personal perspective as we follow Abbiih on her journey of emotional and cognitive healing. I admire her openness and honesty, rare virtues from which we are beneficiaries. Abbiih reveals her scars and challenges us to walk to the healing beat.

As a champion of trauma awareness, prevention, and training, I am always reminded that the thief has come to **kill**, **steal**, and **destroy** (John 10:10), representing the three trauma zones. The enemy wants us to live shadow or pseudo lives that are essentially the products of pervasive, untreated traumas. Furthermore, the rest of the Scripture, "*but I have come that you may have life that is full to overflowing*," gives us a glimpse of God's desire for humanity. We are meant to live life with full cups, but most people live out of half- or quarter-filled cups which only cumulates to frustration and pain. We must become intentional about healing past wounds that keep us from living God destined lives.

Trauma has been well defined in the book, but an unidentified trauma cannot be treated; neither does it go away. Childhood developmental traumas are egregious because they erect faulty foundations for the child's life. Essentially, anything built on these fault lines can be triggered by future interactions. We learn and develop all the schemas necessary to live life during childhood and, if these templates are not constructed properly, we go through adulthood chaotically, trauma prone and relationally deficient. Adverse Childhood Experiences have a close relationship to health and emotional health outcomes in adulthood.

Impacted children will grow up to participate in families, communities, and professions, invariably showing up in these worlds with the impaired functioning and altered personalities formed in their childhood adversities. We must put an end to this terror.

The Lord asked the prophet Jeremiah (8:22), "*Is there no balm in Gilead? Is there no physician there? Why then is there no healing for the wound of my people*?"

Isaiah 42:22 "*But this is a people plundered and looted; they are all of them trapped in holes and hidden in prison; they have become plunder with none to rescue, spoil with none to say, Restore*!"

In my opinion, these two Scripture verses set the stage for Pastor Abbiih's book. There is a balm for all emotional and psychological healing; and therapies are available to unlock prison doors from years past.

Here is an example to explain the concept that untreated trauma doesn't go away, but simply becomes the driver of your life: A couple came for trauma coaching, with the presenting problem that the husband didn't trust his wife although she was not unfaithful. On seeing a man next to her in church, a gathering or even on the bus, he immediately got jealous and frustrated, subjecting her to accusations of cheating and physical abuse. With the marriage on the brink of divorce, they sought our help after years of working with their spiritual leaders.

Our simple inquiry: "when were you first abandoned?" stopped the man in his tracks. He tearfully narrated stories of his father leaving his mother for another woman and how his relatives later abused him as a child. His relational schema was severely ruptured between the ages of 7 and 10. Thirty years later, his wife became the victim of his childhood. Trauma will always rear its head in the present.

Abbiih is an ambassador of healing sent for our times and her book will empower you to deal with long held secrets. You will learn how to release yourself from past traumas and be transformed. Yes, there is a Balm in Gilead.

Happy reading!

Dr. Akindotun Merino
President
Jars Education Group
Mental Health Commissioner
San Bernardino County - 4th District
CEO
African Mental Health Alliance

Section One

Ignorance chips

away at inner peace.

– Abbiih Oloyede

My Journey

I grew up in a household comprising of my mother, father and five siblings. I was the third child. With absolutely no care in the world, growing up and attending primary and secondary school in Lagos, Nigeria, was a fantastic experience. Life was great with no cause for emotional or mental issues.

My teenage years were quite exciting. Dad would arrange for my mum, siblings, and me to go to the theatre to watch Afro-centric movies. Going to the beach was a normal way of having fun in my household. My relationship with my father was brilliant: sitting on his lap telling him stories or asking him for funds to go and buy a nice pair of shoes for him was not unusual. We had an amazing relationship, so his death crushed and shattered my heart into pieces. Also, when he was ill in hospital and wanted to see me, I did not want to speak with him because his health had deteriorated badly, and he had lost so much weight. The thought of him lying there, staring death in the face was unbearable. Little did it occur to me to spend more time with him because he would soon transition to the Land of No Return.

I became a Christian while preparing for my A-levels at one of the Federal Government colleges and went on to attend the University of Lagos, meeting some wonderful people with whom I grew and developed in my Christian faith. Some of them are still a part of my journey today.

My father passed away shortly after being diagnosed with leukaemia, and our entire family became preoccupied with grieving the loss of the patriarch of our home. The September of the year he died (12th July 1985, to be precise) was the same year I gained admission to the University of Lagos.

In my first year, after many invitations from my newly acquired friends, I attended a campus fellowship and began my journey to being a devout Christian. The fellowship's focus on New Creation realities was embedded in all that was said, taught and done. During this time, I fully embraced meditation, studying the word, and living out my new life in Christ. The fellowship leaders also exposed us to myriads of Bible teachers and materials, which was entirely new and exciting. As I reflect on the first time my mind battles began, with hindsight, what I learned during that time helped anchor my mind on the word of God.

After my graduation, my elder brother and sister invited me to further my education by studying for my master's degree in the United Kingdom. On arrival, I stayed with my sister, started attending her church and got involved in the church's prayer ministry.

The first time a stray, troubling thought emerged in my head was during my early twenties. I can vividly remember the sequence. I entered the kitchen to do some menial, forgettable tasks, but the thought and the exact place where 1 was standing is firmly etched on my mind. One minute, I was standing in the kitchen doing some chores, the next, a table knife entered my line of sight, followed by the words:

What if you hurt yourself with this knife?

At first, I did not take notice of the thought and carried on with my chores. However, the bombardment continued, relentlessly telling me to try cutting myself. Before long, the suggestions to hurt myself were so clearly projected that anxiety began to set in. The thoughts became a full-on onslaught, day, and night, and left me clueless about how to handle them.

It never occurred to me to open up to anyone about my state of mind. Mental health issues were foreign territory to me, let alone the existence of thought intrusions, a form of OCD.

> *"Obsessive-compulsive disorder (OCD) is a common mental health condition where a person has obsessive thoughts and compulsive behaviours... If you have OCD, you'll usually experience frequent*

> *obsessive thoughts and compulsive behaviours.* ***An obsession is an unwanted and unpleasant thought, image or urge that repeatedly enters your mind, causing feelings of anxiety, disgust, or unease****. A compulsion is a repetitive behaviour or mental act that you feel you need to do to temporarily relieve the unpleasant feelings brought on by the obsessive thought."*[1]

Further, I was a proud British Nigerian. In the African culture, mental health issues were generally put down to psychosis. In fact, when my dad passed away, even though we were all grief-stricken, no one offered my mother or the children any form of bereavement support or counselling. It was not done at the time.

Each Day was a Battle!

'I do not know what to do about the raging intrusions going through my mind' was the repeated cry of my heart which was full of anxiety. There was no one with whom to discuss my concerns, and the information available was not as robust as it is today.

Then I came across a book called *Right and Wrong Thinking* by a famous Christian writer at the time. In simple terms, he explained the importance of Philippians 4:8 in training the mind. Love Ward, our campus fellowship, had also strongly emphasised studying the scriptures, new creation realities, and habitually speaking God's Word over our lives. Since I did not know what else to do about the thoughts harassing my mind every day, it made sense to memorise Philippians 4:8, confess (speak it out loud) and meditate on it.

Still battling alone, I received a scholarship to attend a Bible School in Cleveland, Tennessee. After settling down at the school, however, the intrusive thoughts gained momentum. One day, it occurred to me to continue with the meditation and proclamation of the Word, this time with greater intensity. Out of desperation and, fed up with the perpetual fear-inducing thoughts, I placed my fingers in my ears and started reciting Philippians 4:8, for anything between 100-200 times a day, for almost four weeks.

A few weeks later, while sitting in a church service, it dawned on me that the thoughts were no longer lingering and nagging like before. I remember trying but failing to call the thoughts to mind. That day, my excitement was untold, and the whole experience became a defining moment in my life that laid the foundation on how to deal with intrusive thoughts. I had gained control and got rid of those thoughts. The fear was gone.

Wow! I had hit on a Mind Jackpot

Other thoughts came and went, but not with the same velocity as before. Over time, it became apparent that fear, anxiety, and intrusions would show up in different seasons and aspects of my life. They still occur today, but the difference is that I know what is happening and have learned to use various tools and tips to bring my mind under control.

One day, after ten years of on and off struggles with these thoughts and anxiety, I was preparing to speak at a Ladies' event. I cannot recall what the conference was about now, but as an avid lover of the Google search engine, I was researching my topic when I came across an article on the mind by the NHS[2]. I could not stop reading until I finished it. It was as though the article's author opened my mind and was writing about my life. The article explained that I was demonstrating symptoms of a mild form of Obsessive-Compulsive disorder produced by what the writer called **thought intrusions.**

> *"Intrusive thoughts are unwanted thoughts that can pop into our heads without warning, at any time. They're often repetitive – with the same kind of thought cropping up again and again – and they can be disturbing or even distressing."* [3]

As I read through the description and ways of addressing the issue, I gradually realised that the thoughts 1 had managed to bring under control using my faith were intrusive, and God's word had been my answer all along. After reading that, I decided Philippians 4:8 would be my mantra. This Bible verse talks about how to train the mind:

> *"Finally, brothers and sisters, whatever is true, whatever is noble, whatever is right, whatever is pure, whatever is lovely, whatever is admirable—if anything is excellent or praiseworthy—* ***think about such things**." (NIV).*

Repeatedly speaking this scripture passage to myself effectively trained my mind to think positively.

Trauma

It is pretty interesting how, after dealing with one mind battle, another emerges. However, struggles in my mind didn't stop me from living my life as a Christian. In the process of serving God, I joined a group of university graduates who gathered every Friday, where I met and fell in love with my husband, Jonathan. After we were married though, I developed the habit of frequently checking whether he was still breathing while he was asleep.

'Abbiih, what is your greatest fear?' He finally asked me one day.

'The thought of you dying!' I replied without hesitation.

'I think you should talk to a therapist,' He suggested in his gentle way.

Thankfully, my friend happens to be a therapist, so I went along to see her.

During our conversation, I realised I was still hugely affected by my father's death. We had such a great relationship that, even as a teenager, I was most comfortable sitting on his lap whenever we talked. The last time I saw him, he had stopped by to visit me at boarding school on his way to a major project he was overseeing in his job as a Chartered Quantity Surveyor.

When I last saw my father, he was hale and hearty, but within a few months, he lay in bed, sick with leukaemia, and died shortly afterwards. My heart was shattered into a thousand pieces. Thankfully,

I had ministered to him, and he became a Christian before he died. After his confession to receive Christ, he told me he felt so at peace.

'Hold on to what you have found, Abbiih,' he told me. 'I spent a tremendous amount of time searching for it.'

His words were part of the reason I clung to my faith in Christ.

My therapist friend was surprised that I grieved my dad for five years, sometimes spending whole days weeping, but the reason for my prolonged grieving soon came to light. During my father's admission to the hospital, he kept asking to see me, but he had lost so much weight and looked very helpless. My 19-year-old heart didn't understand the finality of death, but after his passing, it became clear that he was gone forever, and I would never find out what he wanted to tell me. That overwhelming thought led to five years of crying and grieving. The sessions with my friend helped bring closure to that experience.

Fast forward a few years. During a Trauma-Informed Care Program, I realised the whole incident had traumatised me as well.

> *"Trauma is defined as an emotional response to a terrible event like an accident, loss or natural disaster. Immediately after the event, shock and denial are typical. Longer-term reactions include unpredictable emotions, flashbacks, strained relationships and even physical symptoms like headaches or nausea[4]".*

The trauma addressed; I became fascinated with the mind. After spending countless hours reading online articles, especially those written by psychologists, layers of ignorance began peeling from my mind.

The Temperament

After dealing with the trauma of my father's death, life continued in earnest, and our two exceptional children were born within seven years of each other.

Between raising my children, leading a women's group, speaking at different events and being part of the leadership group at my local church, various elements of my mind battles began to unfold.

One very remarkable one was trying to figure out my identity. It was one I had never contemplated.

I began trying to figure myself out. At the time, it seemed a friend of mine was the best example to emulate. I toned down my dressing into shirts and trousers, which were a far cry from my colourful, adventurous style of dressing that was also reflected in my hairstyles and jewellery. This quest also led me to want to change from being outspoken to becoming quiet, just like my friend. I became reserved, unassuming, non-fashionable, easy-going and laid back because, somewhere in my mind, she was my ideal. I was unaware of myself and my preferences.

Several years later, I organised a meeting called *Step Out to Make a Difference,* to encourage, inspire and motivate women. When it concluded, a member of my team approached me as we were leaving the building and handed me a book.

'Minister Abbiih, I was reading this book, and you came to mind because of the work you do.' she said.

As I scanned through, a light bulb moment occurred. The book contained a temperament test with questions and answers, which I undertook only to discover that I was Sanguine/Melancholic[5]. The revelation of my temperament created an 'aha!' moment for me and, from then on, has been the bedrock for mentally settling my questions about my identity.

Back in university, I had read a book called *Spirit Controlled Temperament* by Tim Lahaye, which went through the different temperament types and how they could affect the way you relate with yourself, others, and God. That book made such an impact on me at the time and may well have been the start of my interest in temperaments and the psychology of the mind.

Temperaments fascinate me mainly because they help me understand why people react the way they do and, consequently, what to do about weak spots in my mind. This stabilised me emotionally and helped me develop self-confidence.

Once I took the test and realised that I am sanguine and melancholic, my extroverted self-returned, complete with dressing in bright colours and enjoying my personality. The awareness of my weaknesses did make me actively work at being a better person.

During this searching period, I became fascinated with articles, workshops, and books on identity. I accepted my personality and temperament but concluded that my identity is first Christian and woman. In addition, everything that has happened to me is part of my story.

The next few years saw me emerging into a much more confident woman who is determined to own her voice, space and who happens to be aware of her strengths, weaknesses, her emotional and mental pattern of thinking, and how she processes information. In other words, I became self-aware.

From my perspective, familiarity with your temperament is the first step towards self-awareness. Today, I use the test extensively in my practice, and anyone I mentor goes through this process. I eventually decided to write this book to help people who struggle with their minds and lack awareness of what it takes to manage their thoughts.

Several factors contribute to mental wellness, and there may be issues that go beyond the scope I will cover here. In some cases, seeing a psychiatrist may be required if you are experiencing severe depression or anxiety. However, I believe you will still find this book helpful.

Next, we will examine wrong thinking, its effect on the healthy mind and how to address the issues that arise. We will also look at the power of God's word to serve as your vitamins or more intensive treatment to keep your mind fit, and, where necessary, effect the healing you will need from the aftermath of intrusive thoughts.

Reflections:

Have you ever experienced thought intrusions?

If you have, what is the nature of the thought/s bombarding your mind?

What sort of emotional reaction/s do you experience?

How do you deal with the thought intrusions?

---

[1] (NHS, n.d.)

[2] (https://www.nhs.uk/mental-health/conditions/obsessivecompulsive-disorder-ocd/overview/#overview)

[3] (What are intrusive thoughts?, n.d.)

[4] (American Psychological Association, n.d.)

[5] To find out more about your temperament, you can take a test the https://www.temperamentquiz.com/ (Bennett, 2022)

Section Two

The best remedy for ignorance is Knowledge. Knowledge makes one confident, bold, and determined to practice what is learnt.

– Abbiih Oloyede

The Healthy Mind

What is Emotional Wellbeing?

Part of the hurdle that required overcoming on my journey to emotional awareness was understanding what constitutes a healthy mind. My quest to acquire knowledge was intense, so I dedicated (mainly) night times when any disturbance was minimal to understanding what was going on with me.

Two popular thoughts nagged at me. The first was a Scripture that says, [6]"My people are destroyed for lack of knowledge", and the other, a saying attributed to Malcolm X: "if you want to hide something from a Black man, write it in a book".

In any event, knowledge gives me the necessary confidence whenever I speak at conferences, seminars, or workshops. Reading psychology magazines, questioning mental health professionals, and Google searches helped me acquire copious information. I began to make sense of thought intrusions and how to put a leash on my mind. What had tormented and created untold anxiety and fear in my life had a name: **Thought Intrusions.**

What does a Healthy Mind look like?

I became eager to not only uncover more about mental and emotional wellbeing but to expressly answer the question: 'What are the signs of a healthy mind?'

I signed up for a Cognitive Behaviour Therapy Practitioner's course and then a course on becoming a Trauma-Informed Care Specialist, followed by an Advanced Trauma Care Practitioner Course. The latter course covered

Dialectical Behaviour Therapy, Couples, Group and Family therapies. These studies gave immense insight into the workings of the mind and how to recognise emotional and mental wellbeing.

The words' emotional' and 'mental' health tend to be swapped with each other; however, they have different meanings. The mind, in its simplest form, is the cognitive part of a human being that facilitates thinking, feeling, remembering, understanding, and reasoning. Based on this simple meaning, the next step would be to explore what the healthy mind looks like. In this chapter, I will try to unpack the following questions:

1. What is mental health?
2. What is emotional health?
3. What does an unhealthy mind look like?

What is Mental Health?

Mental health refers to the ability to handle and manage overwhelming stressors, be productive, relate with others and contribute intentionally to the community. It plays a significant role in the way we think and act and can be categorised into three major parts - social, psychological, and emotional wellbeing. Your mental condition impacts all other areas of your life. The writer of 3 John 2 says: 'I wish above all things that you be in health just as your soul prospers.' [author's paraphrase]

Several elements may affect mental health: including biological/genetic makeup, brain chemistry, life experiences like trauma or abuse, and family hereditary mental health issues.

What is Emotional Health?

Emotional health focuses more on being aware of your feelings and the ability to manage and express them properly. It is the capacity to make use of and practice stress-relieving skills, being capable and flexible enough to appropriately generate feel-good emotions. Emotional health fosters positive moods that lead to healthy relationships with self and others and, in turn, affect productivity levels.

Emotional health tends to affect physical health and vice versa. It is widely accepted that a happy person is likely to end up being successful because of his can-do attitude in finding the necessary tools and creativity to accomplish a task. The energy, optimism, and zest with which he conducts personal, work, or community-related assignments can easily attract others.

A vital precursor to emotional health is possessing the requisite skills to keep the mind in check, some of which are: emotional regulation, distress tolerance, mindfulness, and interpersonal effectiveness.

What does an Unhealthy Mind look like?

There are diverse reasons why the mind can be unhealthy. From a Christian perspective, it is easily traceable to the story of creation and the fall of man in the Garden of Eden.

In the New Testament, Colossians 1:21 (NKJV) says, "*And you, who once were alienated and enemies in your mind by wicked works, yet now He has reconciled*". 1 Corinthians 15:22 goes on to say, "*For as in Adam all die, even so in Christ all shall be made alive.*"

Everyone, regardless of education, creed, culture, and societal status, will battle with their minds at some point. The difference is the level to which the mind interferes with your regular duties or functions. Some people (like me) have weak minds. You will never find me watching horror movies or psychological thrillers because whenever my mind is exposed to such extremities, nightmares and thought projections become an issue. My creative mind begins to daydream about the negative stuff happening to my family members or me.

As I mentioned in the 'what a healthy mind looks like' section above, factors ranging from genes to life experiences to family history can contribute to mental wellbeing. In other words, man's fall resulted in the sinful nature. Some people suffer from physical illnesses and diseases, others predominantly experience mental ill health, while many will experience both in varying degrees. Chronic asthma attacks were a daily occurrence during my childhood, which resulted in countless visits to doctors. It was not until a pastor friend prayed for me that the asthma era ended. After that came the battle of the mind, which continues to date, and I must constantly regulate my emotions and process my thoughts to bring my imagination and thinking to a place of tranquillity and inner calmness.

Some of my clients ask if they will ever get rid of the negative thoughts. I would say, for the most part, if grappling with an aspect of your mind does not stop or hinder you from being productive and getting on with your normal day to day duties, you may be okay. However, if the thought intrusions are overwhelming and you start becoming anxious, then your emotions have become interwoven with the negative thoughts. At this point two things are particularly important:

a) Realising that the thoughts are not yours, and

b) It is an indication of anxiety over anxiety.

Recently, after leading prayer and enjoying fellowship on a ten-day tour of three cities with the other members of our team, I was lying down one night when an avalanche of negative thoughts unexpectedly snowed over my mind. The last time that happened was almost twenty years before. It was so bad that my emotions and thoughts were all over the place. Laying on my bed with palpitations, it occurred to me to reach out to my supervisor for support. Thankfully, she wasn't in any session, so she explained what had happened, and what was going on, and reminded me of what to do, which included:

a) Breathing

b) Reminding myself that they were just thoughts

c) That anxiety was playing out

d) Taking a warm, then cold bath to calm my nerves

e) Using mindfulness as a form of grounding and being in the present.

The entire experience reinforced to me that the mind can do what it wills at any time, and one must be prepared for such eventualities. The phenomena led me to delve more into thought intrusions and to read up to date information on dealing with such interruptions.

Thoughts are what they are – spontaneous, free flowing ideas, opinions, queries, assumptions, and ideologies that enter the conscious mind unannounced. Our response to them is the most important aspect of dealing with intrusive thoughts. From my perspective, anxiety, and fear, depending on the severity of the image, can determine what happens next, and understanding this gives me inner peace and calmness. Also, allowing the thoughts to float away just as they floated into my mind really helps. In the past, my strategy was to consciously attempt to interrupt the thoughts, not realising that this approach simply made matters worse. Recognising that my mind is **sticky** and my battle with the mind is genetic has been useful when putting my experience into perspective.

Stickiness of mind is the term used to define,

> *"a biologically based trait that is experienced as repetitive looping thinking, a sense of getting mired in worry, a talent for imaginative flights into catastrophic images and thoughts, and a tendency for junk channels of the mind to get loud and insistent instead of simply flowing by. It is highly heritable, so it tends to run in families, and it is sensitive to stress such as fatigue, illness, or chronic conflict. It also increases with positive stress like excitement. Stickiness is not a sign of mental illness: it is a*

> *characteristic that, once understood, can be incorporated into a full and meaningful life"* [7].

Now that you and I know what a healthy mind looks like, I suggest using the above as your basis to assess your mental and emotional health and wellbeing on a scale of 1-10. Once you have done this, you can begin the process and commitment to change.

Reflections:

How healthy is your mind?

Result

Reasons for saying you have a healthy or unhealthy mind

Take a moment to pause, get into a comfortable posture, relax, and meditate on your answers. Jot down steps you will take to improve your thought life. Remember your brain has the capacity to heal!!

---

[6] Hosea 4:6

[7] (Psy.D., 2019)

Section Three

There is nothing you have been through that cannot be healed because the mind has the capacity to be retrained.

– Abbiih Oloyede

Anyone Can Change

Ignorance is quite costly. In the early days of grappling with severe tormenting thought intrusions, it never occurred to me to seek help, for a combination of factors including:

- The stigma attached to seeing a doctor about issues to do with my mind
- The thought of any visits being placed on my medical record and
- My ability to gain employment could potentially be stifled by the misinformation that the condition meant psychosis.

First and foremost, my life is proof that God's word has the power to calm the mind and overcome negative thoughts. Secondly, the depth of knowledge I acquired (and am still acquiring) in the process of trying to get a complete grip on my mind is incredible. So is helping whoever may be experiencing relational growth issues with themselves, others, and their spirituality.

Getting the mind to toe the line must be done intentionally. People think it is a one-off project, but I came to realise that the mind is like a child wandering off into thought intrusions, doubt, low self-esteem, anxiety and much more. The will, on the other hand, is the parent who gently guides the mind towards hope, calmness, joy, confidence, and positive thinking.

A leading psychologist, Dr Henry Cloud, once said on one of his social media platforms, "A leopard can't change its spots - we are not leopards. We are people, and people change.

People change through growth, repentance, learning and feedback[8]."

For some reason, that redefined famous adage struck a chord with me. We are humans and not animals, and we have the cognitive ability to think, assess and, depending on the sort of change needed, make up our minds to change. Having said that, the commitment and determination to reframe or renew the mind is not child's play. A man's will only takes him so far. Support therapy, counselling, coaching, mentoring can help. For the person of faith, prayer and meditation will also boost the desired mind transformation.

Commitment

The dictionary defines commitment as 'the state or quality of being dedicated to a cause.' One thing that is very real to me is the price required for inner peace. We also see that 2 Corinthians 10:5 refers to '*casting down imaginations*'. To cast down is to take down forcefully. It is to throw or pull down and demolish.[9]

To win the battle of the mind, you must be prepared to win the war against your thoughts and/or imaginations. The following proverbs describe man's propensity towards as well as the effect of wrong thinking and imaginations:

> *'...for their hearts devise violence, and their lips declare trouble.'*
> *Proverbs 24:2 BSB*
> *'A heart that devises wicked plans....'*
> *Proverbs 6:18*
> *'The heart is deceitful above all things, and desperately wicked: who can know it?' Jeremiah 17:9*

It has taken a lot of personal commitment to reach the place where my thoughts and heart's wicked imaginations do not control my actions, even if the thoughts and negative imaginations are overwhelming.

The other day, my daughter and I went out to watch a movie. I settled down with a large sweet and salty popcorn, my large drink, and a straw. As we waited patiently for the film to start, an annoying negative thought suddenly popped into my mind. It was annoying because it had absolutely nothing to do with what was on the screen. If you have battled with your mind, you will be aware that just as headaches strike unannounced, inexplicable thoughts can sneakily spring into the mind. This is why you must plan and practice the relevant skills to keep your mind in check by demolishing those imaginations.

Addressing Mental Health Problems

God gives human beings the wisdom to unpack and understand why people act the way they do, and the best way to remedy the problems we encounter. One of the things that struck me during session after session with those who approached me for emotional or mental support is the need to categorise and often be able to tell why the person is behaving and reacting to an emotional or mental issue. I believe this influenced the development of the different interventions that can be used to bring peace to the mind, thoughts, and eventually emotional/ mental responses. It's the reason certifications and trainings are paramount, as one can use the tried and tested methods to deal with mental/emotional agonies. With so much research and different branches of psychology, it's worth giving a summary of the three principal areas of mental and emotional interventions:

a) **Psychology**: deals with the study of the mind and how we behave, and it explores a variety of treatments for mental, emotional, and behavioural induced disorders.

b) **Psychiatry:** focuses more on the diagnosis and treatment of mental health issues

c) **Psychotherapy**: focuses more on using various psychological methods, rather than medicine, to treat emotional, mental, and behavioural disorders. That said, some psychology clinicians do prescribe medication.

One thing that comes to mind, when reflecting on the three primary areas of study stated above, is the good news for Christians that the tools required for renovating your soul and mine are readily available and can be found in the Scriptures. In fact, I daresay that most processes used to alleviate emotional and mental stress form part of many Christians' day-to-day routines. For example, daily devotions can overhaul negative mindsets and praying and being quiet are forms of meditation and mindfulness. You can distract the mind by listening to music, dancing is quite therapeutic, and assembling with people of like mind is effectively belonging to a support network. The list is endless. I believe God got there before man, and man is now unravelling the tips and tools engineered perfectly by the Creator.

CBT and DBT

Two main processes that I use and frequently find helpful are: Cognitive Behaviour Therapy and Dialectical Behaviour Therapy. Both skills emphasise why personal daily devotions are important to the Christian.

Cognitive Behavioural Therapy (CBT)

According to the NHS:

> *"CBT is based on the concept that your thoughts, feelings, physical sensations and actions are interconnected, and that negative thoughts and feelings can trap you in a vicious cycle. CBT aims to help you deal with overwhelming problems in a more positive way by breaking them down into smaller parts. You're shown how to change these negative patterns to*

improve the way you feel. Unlike other talking treatments, CBT deals with your current problems rather than focusing on issues from your past. It looks for practical ways to improve your state of mind on a daily basis."[10]

Dialectical Behaviour Therapy (DBT)

No one glove fits all when it comes to dealing with mental and emotional challenges. However, the four primary skills, heralded as most effective, fall under what is known as Dialectical Behaviour Therapy.

"The goal of DBT is to help you "break free" of seeing the world, your relationships and your life in a very narrow, rigid way that leads you to engage in harmful and self-destructive behaviour.... [and] to break this cycle by introducing two important concepts:

- Validation – accepting that your emotions are valid, authentic, and acceptable

- Dialectics – a school of philosophy that says most things in life are rarely "black or white" and that it's essential to be open to ideas and opinions that contradict your own".[11]

DBT was developed by Marsha Linehan, a practitioner who established the program due to her personal experience of mental illness and the treatments she received. Introduced in the eighties, DBT is used to treat a range of disorders, from eating to borderline personality disorders. After being diagnosed with Schizophrenia, Marsha

Linehan underwent all the usual treatments, which ranged from medication to electroshock treatment to being sectioned by the age of eighteen.

A psychologist by profession, Linehan concluded that she had been misdiagnosed. In addition, as a long-standing practising Roman Catholic, Marsha practised meditation as taught by the monks, leading to a very positive experience with mindfulness (which is at the core of DBT). In practice, DBT validates the patient's feelings while also helping them realise that certain feelings and behaviours aren't beneficial, teaching them better alternatives[12].

When DBT was introduced during my Advanced Integrated Behavioural Counselling Certification program, it was an immediate love affair that revolutionised my skills. Now let's unravel the four building blocks of DBT.

Distress Tolerance Skills have to do with an individual's ability to manage and get a grip in moments of real or imagined emotional stress. It is drawing on your ability to be rational and resilient in stressful situations without making the issue worse or letting things get out of hand. The following story highlights a few strategies for dealing with a distressing situation.

In the Bible, David goes off to war with his men and returns home to be confronted with an invasion of his city's commerce and the capture of their wives and children. The shock created an instant reaction of tears and hopelessness in his men, however, David spent time meditating, praying, and seeking God's guidance. He soon received an assurance that yes, he should go and recover what had been taken off them, and what was lost was restored[13].

Mindfulness: A buzzword that has recently emerged is mindfulness, described as being present with your thoughts. It is taking the time to evoke a word, thought or action to calm and relieve the mind from internal or external pressures. Mindfulness puts whatever you may be experiencing emotionally or mentally into context, using your senses.

Emotional Regulation: Emotions, which we all have, are signals telling us what's happening within the body. When something pleasing happens, you feel great, while an unpleasant occurrence can make you sad and unhappy. Your emotions are like an instant news reporter...breaking news. They play a critical role in how you live, from influencing your day-to-day engagement with others to affecting your decision-making.

Interpersonal Effectiveness has to do with what I refer to as relational dynamics. It focuses on being able to interact with other people and gives tips and tools on how we come across so we can manage our interactions. It includes but is not limited to verbal and non-verbal communication, assertiveness, problem solving, decision making, listening and being able to negotiate your thoughts, feelings, and actions.

How Widespread are Mental Health Problems?

A study[14] conducted by Mind (a UK charity that provides advice and support for anyone experiencing mental health problems) states that one in four people will experience a mental health problem of some kind each year and one in six will report experiencing common mental health issues like anxiety and depression in any given week in England (see article for more figures)[15]. Some people are diagnosed with different conditions over time.

The spectrum is vast, but I will briefly mention suicidal thoughts and self-harm, which are related to mental health but not diagnosed as such. It is said that a high number of the population has suicidal thoughts, self-harm, and attempt suicide[16]. A study by McManus S, Bebbington P, Jenkins R, Brugha T. (eds.) (2016) states that while women are more likely to have suicidal thoughts, more men go further to attempt to take their own lives[17].

The ratio of adults suffering from mental health problems who seek or receive treatment is 1 in 8, of which the majority are offered psychiatric medication. It is also reported that the number of people suffering with mild to severe mental problems in England and Wales has seen a steady increase in recent years, as have suicide and self-harming numbers.

The Mind article further states that while mental health problems can happen to anyone, groups such as LGBTIQ+, Black or Black British people, and those with issues like homelessness, substance abuse, etc., may also be predisposed to mental health issues. Those facing societal disadvantages, including discrimination, inequality, exclusion, and people who have suffered trauma and severe physical health problems may also be at risk of mental ill-health.

Reflections:

Do you believe you can change the way you think? Be honest.

Result

Reasons for saying you can and cannot

Take a moment to pause, get into a comfortable posture, relax, and meditate on your answers. Jot down steps you will take to improve your thought life. Remember your brain has the capacity to heal!!

---

[8] (Cloud)

[9] https://www.blueletterbible.org/lexicon/g2507/kjv/tr/0-1/

[10] (NHS, n.d.)

[11] (NHS, n.d.)

[12] https://www.delraycenter.com/3-interesting-facts-about-the-creator-of-dbt/

[13]1 Samuel 30

[14] (MIND, 2020)

[15] https://www.mind.org.uk/information-support/types-of-mental-health-problems/statistics-and-facts-about-mental-health/how-common-are-mental-health-problems/#References

[16] Ibid.

[17] Mental health and wellbeing in England: Adult psychiatric morbidity survey 2014.

Section Four

Intrusive thoughts are intruders to the mind that feed on anxiety. Remember this: they are just thoughts, nothing more, nothing less.

– Abbiih Oloyede

Thought Intrusions

The thing about thoughts is: everyone has them. We all have upsetting or strange thoughts, and, sometimes, they do not make a lot of sense.

Guess what? **This is normal**.

In fact, several well-conducted studies have discovered that almost 100% of the general population has intrusive and disturbing thoughts, disturbing images, or ideas. If any of the three applies to you, you are not alone. I have been there too.

My first thought intrusions episode happened in my early 20's. It was so unexpected and horrible. The thought came as a *whoosh*! and **my emotional reaction made the thought stick**. One way of addressing these intrusions is to recognise that they are just junk thoughts and nothing more. However, your reaction will determine whether they stick or float away.

In my case, the violent nature of the thought made me extremely anxious, and anxiety feeds junk thoughts. At first, I did not know what to do, but thankfully, the university fellowship I attended had placed considerable emphasis on the art of meditation. When the negative thoughts bombarded my mind, I used the weapon of meditating on and confessing the scriptures to reframe my thoughts and bring my mind to a place of peace.

Psalm 94:19 says, '*in the multitude of my anxieties within me, your comforts delight my soul*' (NKJV). From my personal journey, managing my mind has been a combination of the word and scientific understanding, which is what I share today as I teach my clients to do the same. After being strengthened, I can strengthen others.

Say this to yourself:

> *I am not my thoughts!*
> *I can control my thoughts.*
> *Thought intrusions are junk thoughts!*
> *I have the mind of Christ.*

Junk Thoughts

One of the ways of managing and understanding thought intrusions is by consciously designating them as junk thoughts, because that is what they are. Simply put, they are rubbish, garbage, waste, dross thoughts that float through the mind. Thought intrusions are:

- Unwanted inserted whoosh! *junk* thoughts.
- Unwanted *junk* thoughts
- Involuntary, unexpected *junk* thoughts

Unwanted images, phrases, or impulses are common attributes of thought intrusions.

There are some signs to look out for if you are experiencing intrusive thoughts.

- If the thoughts are unusual thoughts that are not characteristic of your character and very different from how you typically think. Most likely you are dealing with a thought intrusion. Sometimes they can be spontaneous thoughts of violence towards children, yourself, loved ones or even animals. They could be about inappropriate sexual contact or even blasphemous words floating through your consciousness.

- Intrusive thoughts are not necessarily sinful—even blasphemous ones. They could be spiritual, where you think to yourself- *God doesn't love me, I am not a good Christian. I am going to hell,* etc. These extreme thoughts cause some people to question their salvation, integrity, character, and sanity.

- If the thought is bothersome, disturbing and something you want to push out of your mind, it might be an intrusive thought.

- If the thought feels hard to control, is repetitive and won't go away. The more you dwell on it, the more anxious you become and the worse the thoughts get. That is an intrusive thought.

The best way to deal with an intrusive thought is to STOP fighting. Adjust and take the following steps:

1. Identify the thought. Tell yourself, 'That's just an intrusive thought. It's not how I think, it's not what I believe, and it's not what I want to do.

2. Don't fight it. Accept it for what it is (intrusive), and allow it to float away the way it floated in. Don't try to make it go away.

3. Don't judge yourself. Having a strange or disturbing thought doesn't indicate that something is wrong with you.

"Therefore gird up the loins of your mind, be sober, and rest your hope fully upon the grace that is to be brought to you at the revelation of Jesus Christ."
(1 Peter 1:13)

The Thought Exercise

Thoughts really do play games on us! In my practice, I sometimes conduct timed exercises, where clients write down every thought that goes through their mind in three minutes. The first time I did the exercise myself, I had 90 thoughts in three minutes. Multiply that by 20 minutes. 1,800 thoughts floated through my mind in one hour! If

I stayed awake for 7 hours, that's 12,600 thoughts in one day.

That life-saving exercise further emphasised the fact that all kinds of thoughts will float through the mind, good and bad! So don't beat yourself up!

Here are a few things you can do to lift any form of guilt or anxiety you may experience.

Memorise the scriptures and pray. If these two practices do not diminish harmful thoughts and inclinations, the body's own chemistry may be at work. Intrusive thoughts are sometimes a symptom of obsessive-compulsive disorder, post-partum depression, and attention deficit disorder, among other things.

Do not despair; you are not alone!

Just as God provided trained professionals to advise in spiritual matters, he has provided practitioners who can help with managing the mind. Cognitive Behaviour Therapy, for instance, is used mainly to manage thought intrusions, especially when the thoughts become debilitating.

'Anxiety in the heart of man causes depression, but a good word makes it glad' (Proverbs 12:25). The good word can be from you recognising that the thought is junk, or sitting with a practitioner who talks you through your fears.

Peace of Mind

> *"I am leaving you with a gift—peace of mind and heart. And the peace I give is a gift the world cannot give. So don't be troubled or afraid."* John 14:27 NIV

Peace here refers to tranquillity, calmness, contentment or quiet. It is freedom from disquieting or oppressive thoughts and emotions. Attaining peace of mind requires your full attention. You must do the work of peace.

The opposite of peace is stress.

Stress is mental or emotional strain or tension resulting from adverse or demanding circumstances. We all get stressed, and right now, there's so many reasons to be stressed. However, as Ralph Waldo Emerson says, "Nobody can bring you peace but yourself."

Let me share a few tips on how to bring yourself to a place of inner peace and tranquillity:

Speedily accepting God's sovereignty on a matter is so important. God's conclusion on a matter, situation or circumstance may not be in line with your expectation.

End your thoughts with hope, no matter how dire the situation. Intentionally bring your thoughts to a place of assurance. Don't leave negative thoughts hanging loosely in your mind.

Maintain an attitude of hope. '*Be thankful in all circumstances, for this is God's will for you who belong to Christ Jesus.*' 1 Thessalonians 5:18 NLT

Practise mindfulness (being in the present). For example, you have just lost your precious job or suddenly receive news that you will be made redundant. Panic, anxiety, confusion, and worry may overwhelm your mind as you think of your bills and responsibilities. As you muse on what tomorrow may bring and what to do next. Say to yourself right now, 'I am here. I have experience and am qualified to get another job. When one door shuts, another will open.' You can then sit in a comfortable position and try relaxing your mind and body. Doing this not only calms the mind and nerves down, but regularly practising it may even help your creativity to flow. Tell yourself, '**I can do this**'!

Thought Intrusions and The Prophetic

> *"Give a man a word from God and he's inspired for a day. Teach a man to hear from God and he's inspired for a lifetime." Mike Vikler*[18]

Thought intrusions come to us through the same channel as the impressions and nudges from the Holy Spirit.

As one who has worked through both intrusions and prophetic words, my ability to discern has developed through practise. Prophetic words tend to come very quietly, followed by calmness. Thought intrusions, on the other hand, are accompanied by terror and really bad pictures; and the emotions that follow are anxiety, nervousness, and fear.

That said, I always subject every word I hear to God's word. Depending on the situation, if no Scripture verse follows, it takes a while for me to release the impression or prophetic word. Once, while praying with someone, I saw a child running up and down. I weighed it in my heart and then explained what I saw. The individual was so excited. They had a desire to have children and started intentionally praying towards it.

> *"My sheep hear My voice, and I know them, and they follow Me. And I give them eternal life, and they shall never perish; neither shall anyone snatch them out of My hand. My Father, who has given them to Me, is greater than all; and no one is able to snatch them out of My Father's hand. I and My Father are one."* John 10: 27-30 NKJV

The voice and presence of God usually come with love, kindness, patience, calmness, hope. He is reassuring, forgiving, encouraging, peaceful, gentle, and comforting. The voice of the enemy/flesh is full of guilt, condemnation, judgement, punishment, hopelessness, anxiety, haste, and destruction.

The spirit of prophecy is the testimony of Jesus, so prophetic words should lead you and me more towards Christ. They should edify, encourage, and comfort.

Practising meditation and reading the word is very important for anyone who dreams, sees visions, and receives heavenly downloads. Delivering the word with wisdom is so important as well. These help me stay grounded.

My Inner Thoughts

Everyone has two major stories playing in their minds. One is **about** our life, the other **controls** our life. The story that controls your life is where you create in your mind what it means to be you. A way to understand your internal monologue is to complete the following sentence three times: "I am the sort of person who…" Then write it down.

For instance, if you wrote that you would like to be more vocal at work or with your spouse, focus on the contexts in which you would like to be more vocal, how you feel when you keep quiet, and what you could do differently. Becoming more vocal is about trusting yourself.

Did you ever realize that everything going on in your mind—every thought, feeling, sensation, everything you are aware of—is in fact happening only in your private internal world? We are aware of our thoughts, so they are real to us, yet, they do not exist elsewhere. The thought appearing to you at this moment is not occurring anywhere else.

Your inner story follows you around from the moment you wake up until you go to bed. The minute you wake up, the thoughts start and continue all through the day. It is not unusual for between 7000 and 10,000 thoughts to pass through our minds daily. The more we read, engage with the news, the word, music, and interact with people, the more we fill our subconscious mind with information which will then be presented to us as thoughts.

You may not be able to control the thoughts that pop into your mind, but you can challenge and direct them, switch a negative for a positive, and work on the inner story you tell yourself.

Some people's inner story has been traumatised by their childhood or relationships, so they find it difficult to change what they say and think about themselves.

> *'We use our powerful Christ-tools for smashing warped philosophies, tearing*

> *down barriers erected against the truth of God, fitting every loose thought and emotion and impulse into the structure of life shaped by Christ. Our tools are ready at hand for clearing the ground of every obstruction and building lives of obedience into maturity'* (2 Cor 5:4-6 The Message).

You can change your inner narration. The beauty of humanity is that because of neuroplasticity, there is no trauma you have experienced that can't be healed. But you must be prepared to do the mind work; no one can do it for you. Neuroplasticity is the brain's ability to adapt to changes in your environment by forming new neural connections over time. Neuroplasticity explains how the human brain can adapt, master new skills, store memories and information and even recover after a traumatic brain injury.

Tongue and Thoughts

> *"Likewise, the tongue is a small part of the body, but it makes great boasts. Consider what a great forest is set on fire by a small spark. The tongue also is a fire, a world of evil among the parts of the body. It corrupts the whole body, sets the whole course of one's life on fire, and is itself set on fire by hell."* James 3:5-6 NIV

The ability to control, influence and tame the tongue requires you to prepare for the unavoidable. I suggest you practice well in advance so that, when the situation arises, your subconscious mind comes to the rescue and can then control the situation before your conscious mind kicks in. That's because we react from our subconscious.

Here are a few practical tips to help tame the tongue.

Some people tend to put their foot in their mouth when they are nervous, or the situation seems urgent. Even if you jump the gun and have started reacting, do the following:

a) CALM DOWN: Calming down can help you control your tongue. If nervousness makes you say things that you may later regret, then take a few deep breaths. Imagine things going well, being relaxed and in control of yourself and your tongue.

b) PAUSE: taking a deep breath and counting to 10, or pausing for 10 seconds before you speak, can be beneficial. This will give you time to think. If you can make sense of what you want to say, then go ahead. If not, keep quiet.

   Sometimes the person is waiting on your response, and 10 seconds can make for an awkward pause. Take at least three seconds to consider your words before you respond.

   Remember to take the 10-second pause before you post, comment, or reply to things online. Make sure what you are posting isn't something that you might regret later.

c) Consider the consequences. Take a moment to think about the effect your words could have on the other person and situation. Tap into your empathy and ask yourself, "How would I feel if someone said this to me?", or "What feelings might this comment bring up for the other person?" Realizing the embarrassment and damage your words can cause is one way to learn to hold them in.

Words can hurt and, even though they forgive you, people remember how you made them feel. They might not say anything right then, but it could damage your relationship.

d) Think it but don't say it. Everyone has thought something negative or mean about someone or a situation at some point. It's natural. You can think whatever you want; the problems only start once those thoughts become words that hurt others. Control your tongue by only saying what is appropriate.

If you can't think of anything positive to say, smile politely, nod, and subtly change the subject.

Reflections:

Do the three-minute thought test, so you have an idea of the number of thoughts that flows in and out of your mind daily.

Result

What is the predominant thought you grapple with daily?

What story do you tell yourself?

Do you believe you can change the story you are telling yourself?

Reasons for saying yes/no

Take a moment to pause, get into a comfortable posture, relax, and meditate on your answers. Jot down steps you will take to improve your thought life. Remember your brain has the capacity to heal!!

---

[18] https://awakenedto.life/4-keys-class/

Section Five

Conviction without corresponding action is a waste of time. Do the mind work!

– Abbiih Oloyede

The Mind Work

The saying, 'Man is a spirit, he has a soul and lives in a body' is a simple way of understanding the human makeup. Most Christians, including me, believe that when you receive Christ (when you believe and confess that Jesus Christ is the son of God and that he came to the world to die for your sins), your spirit is converted, and you become a child of God.

When conversion takes place, your spirit is regenerated, and it becomes the bridge through which you relate with the spirit world. The human spirit is also the avenue by which you pick up on heavenly thoughts and impressions (known as prophetic insights). The same spirit embodies the soul so that, at the time of death, your spirit and soul leave, and your body becomes lifeless. In the

Garden of Eden, God breathed into man's nostrils, and he became a living soul (Genesis 2:7). When man sinned, as God had forewarned[19], he died.

When Adam fell, the entire human race (and I dare say every human soul) was launched into an unending battle of the spirit, soul, and body. Much as God loved Adam and Eve, he did not tamper with their will when they went off track. He had given clear cut instructions on what to do and what not to do, and He will not strive with man's will (Genesis 6:3). However, in Christ, we experience the new creation realities, and can now put on the new man.

> *"But you have not so learned Christ, if indeed you have heard Him and have been taught by Him, as the truth is in Jesus: that you put off, concerning your*

> *former conduct, the old man, which grows corrupt according to the deceitful lusts, and* ***be renewed in the spirit of your mind, and that you put on the new man*** *which was created according to God, in true righteousness and holiness."* Ephesians 2:20-24

'*Ananeoō*', the Greek word for 'renewed' in this passage, means to renovate, renew, reform. To be renewed in your mind is to be spiritually transformed, to take on a new mind. The word 'spirit' (*Pneuma* in Greek) refers, among other things, to the human soul, which possesses the power of knowing, desiring, deciding, and acting. According to the Blue Letter Bible[20], *Pneuma* can refer to a life-giving spirit as well as the human soul that has left the body. The Greek word for soul found in Genesis 2:7 is *Nous,* which refers to the disposition or influence governing a person and their source of power, affection, emotion, desire.

In other words, Ephesians 2:23 is saying you and I have the responsibility to renovate and renew our God-given human souls. This means the mind's renovation – cleaning, repairing, rebuilding, renewing, and overhauling – is something we can commit to and, by so doing, restore it to a place of peace, vigour, or activity.

Other synonyms for 'renew' range from restoration to reconstruction – basically, you are giving your soul a complete makeover.

> *"For the life of the flesh is in the blood, and I have given it to you upon the altar*

to make atonement for your souls; for it is the blood that makes atonement for the soul." Leviticus 17:11

"Therefore, if any ***man*** *be in Christ, he is a* ***new*** *creature: old things are passed away; behold, all things are become* ***new****."* 2 Corinthians 5:17

"...and that you ***put on the new man*** *which was created according to God, in true righteousness and holiness."* Ephesians 4:24

Understanding that Christ is the doorway to a sound, renewed mind and emotional peace will give you the faith to confidently do the mind work.

The Word and Mind Work

From a Christian perspective, the following Scripture passages run parallel to the tools for effective mind transformation. Let's paraphrase the verses so you can see how they can apply to you:

Matthew 6:22 - "*Your eye is the lamp of your body. If your eye is single (*good and healthy*), your whole body shall be full of light.*" In other words, your mind is the window by which you see things and there is a connection between what you are focusing on and your body's reaction. The mind and body are like twins, feeding off each other. 3 John 2, which says: "*I wish above all things that you prosper and be in health as your soul prospers*" also comes to mind here.

Isaiah 26:3 - "God will keep you in perfect peace when your mind is stayed on Him because you trust in Him."

Matthew 6:31 - "*Therefore, **take** no thought, **saying**....*"

Mark 11:23 – "*If you **say** to this mountain, 'Be removed and be cast into the sea,' and do not **doubt** in your heart, but **believe** that those things you say will be done, you will have whatever you say.*"

Psalm 27:12 – "*...I would have lost heart unless I had believed that I would see the goodness of the Lord in the land of the living....*"

The Finished Work of Christ

The suggested starting point for transforming the mind is the Cross, where Jesus said, 'it is finished!'

and the curtain ripped into two[21]. The words 'It is finished!' mean the spiritual work for my salvation (*Sozo*) has been concluded and can be appropriated to my mind. 1 Thessalonians 5:23 puts it this way:

"Now may the God of peace make you holy in every way and may your whole spirit and soul and body be kept blameless until our Lord Jesus Christ comes again."

Meditating on the Word

> *Finally, brethren, whatever things are true, whatever things are noble, whatever things are just, whatever things are pure, whatever things are lovely, whatever things are of good report, if there is any virtue and if there is anything praiseworthy—meditate on these things.* Philippians 4:8

The campus fellowship, my home for the three years while studying for my degree program, placed considerable emphasis on the new creation realities, which really helped me grow and develop in my Christian walk.

Part of the discipline taught by the leaders was using Bible dictionaries to further understand the context and the varied meaning of words when studying the Word. So, when it became clear that thought intrusions were a problem, my first port of call was to find out what the Scriptures said about dealing with mind issues, with Philippians 4:8 being my go-to for solace and mind encouragement.

It made so much sense to dedicate time to unpack the verse. As previously mentioned, the exercise was beneficial, and the thought intrusions stopped.

Three decades later, if my mind wants to wander off course or, the minute a negative thought starts dancing around in my mind, the verse automatically pops up in my head, immediately making me calm.

The following are the steps I used to embed Philippians 4:8 in my mind.

- Memorise the entire verse by cramming it – open the Bible to read the passage repeatedly.

- Shut the Bible and recite the verse, and then cross-check to make sure it was verbatim.

- Poke my fingers into both ears and recite the verse with my eyes closed (at the peak of it, fifty to a hundred times, up to five times a day).

- Go to the church hall or retreat area (in other words, find a quiet place) to conduct the above exercises.

Fear tormented me each time and created palpitations. However, my resilience made me keep engaging in church services without telling anyone what was going on since there were no professionals around to guide me through how to deal with the intrusions. Four weeks later, the thoughts were no longer flooding my mind, and the peace experienced was such a surprise to me. Then I continued practising meditation and calling the Scripture to remembrance without having to place my fingers in my ears.

The actions described above are a form of meditation, cognitive rehearsal and rewiring of my thought processing to give me great inner peace. The knowledge acquired during my training has equipped me to comfortably deal with thought intrusions. The Bible also has so many techniques and tools for a sound and calm mind, several of which overlap with exercises recommended by other practitioners as a way of dealing with mental and emotional stress. To mention a few:

> Isaiah 26:3 – '*He keeps in peace whose mind is stayed on him.*' [author's paraphrase]
>
> Joshua 1:8 - '*This Book of the Law shall not depart from your mouth, but you shall meditate in it day and night, that you may observe to do according to all that is written in it. For then, you will make your way*

prosperous, and then you will have good success.

Psalm 77:6 - '*I call to remembrance my song in the night; I meditate within my heart, And my spirit makes diligent search.'*

Hardness of Heart

For the mind work to be effective and yield the desired result over time, you and I must be aware of what is in our hearts. Jeremiah 17:9 says, *"The heart is deceitful above all things, and desperately wicked; who can know it?"*

The heart of man, as described in the Scriptures, represents man's thought patterns, appetites, desires, intelligence, creativity, mental and emotional processing. The heart took a downward spiral when Adam and Eve sinned in the Garden of Eden. Jesus came to redeem us; however, you and I will find that the things we want to do, we do not do and that which we have no business doing, we catch ourselves doing. Once we have this understanding, we must be willing to put in the necessary mind work to experience the finished work of the Cross.

The Greek word for hardness of heart is *sklerokardia.* It is used three times in the New Testament. First, when Jesus tells off his disciples for not believing:

> *'Later He appeared to the eleven as they sat at the table; and He rebuked their unbelief and hardness of heart, because they did not believe those who had seen Him after He had risen.* Mark 16:14

The second time was in Mark 10:5 when he was explaining Moses' rationale behind divorce, and then once more in Romans 2:5 when Paul the Apostle draws our attention to living righteously by practising what we preach.

I believe hardness of heart stems from one or more of the following traits. A hard heart:

- Is devoid of the word of God.
- Has decided to do things her own way regardless of what the Bible says on a matter.
- May have been traumatised and finds it hard to respond to the wisdom of the Word.

- Will not yield to the wisdom of those who, by reason of age, can discern right from wrong.

- Will not respond to the voice of a professional, mentor, coach, etc., due to Adverse Childhood Experiences.

Our upbringing and childhood experiences shape our outlook. More pertinently, thoughts that stem from our hearts will influence the way we behave and respond to situations and circumstances, which, in turn, dramatically affects our emotions.

Most of the time, the state of your heart is fully unveiled when you start engaging in relationships. For me, marriage was the platform through which my strengths and weaknesses came on full display. Certain experiences made me realise I had to try and understand my reactions and behaviours and to gain more insight into my thinking patterns. As a new bride, within weeks of saying “I do” to Jonathan, my darling husband, my constant mood swings became quite evident. My sanguine (impulsive, spontaneous) and melancholic (perfectionist, depressive and emotional) traits were always at play. Jonathan’s choleric (leader, structured and must-do-now) nature made him engage in regular intense conversations with me. At one point, he desperately pleaded with me to try adjusting my facial expressions and attitudes, to prevent family and friends from misunderstanding me.

After more than two decades of being married, gaining my CBT Practitioner qualification, and running Trauma-Informed and Advance Integrated Behavioural Certification programs with my clients, I have a great understanding of the state of my heart, my personal perspectives, and most significantly, various vital techniques to ensure my heart is in the right place. Depending on the situation, I employ CBT skills to unravel limiting beliefs and interchangeably use the four primary DBT skills to maintain healthy relationships with myself, my husband, family, friends, etc.

Jonathan always says, when a thought, impression or feeling surfaces, do not repress it. Press in to gain an insight into the 'what' and 'why' of your thoughts. A few years ago, I remember waking up and wondering whether the constant irritation, mood swings and the resulting emotional isolation could be eliminated by following his advice. The time spent meditating and teasing out the thoughts eventually highlighted my state of mind. From then until now, the changes in my emotions and mental processing have been immense.

With the experience and knowledge acquired over time, it aches me to see individuals, couples, old and young adults, and children undergoing any emotional or mental pain. If it were possible, everyone who steps into my practice or life would end up with a transformed mind. However, for the transition to take place, each person must be willing to do the mind work. It takes consistent time and effort for most people to understand the battle of the mind and to then commit to the journey to emotional wholeness.

Being born again is step one of this journey. Step two is developing emotional and mental wellbeing.

Emotional Wellbeing

When an individual has the capacity to use stress management techniques, he is strong and tough enough to produce, as and when needed, the emotions that help him thrive in good and tough times, knowing, understanding and utilising the right strategies. Emotional wellbeing helps the person relate with himself and the community at large.

To develop your emotional wellbeing, it is crucial that you invest time, and sometimes money, to acquire, practice and put in place the necessary emotional and mental skills to help you undergo challenging times and situations. Now let us examine some of the said tips and tools.

More on Therapeutic Interventions

From my perspective, communication is one of the fundamental ways by which most human beings can describe their emotions, thoughts, behaviours, and feelings. These are generally referred to as **talk therapies**.

Talk therapy is when an individual seeks emotional or mental support from a trained practitioner. There are different ways of referring to such individuals: counsellors, therapists, psychotherapists, to mention a few. The aim is to sit down with someone who will listen to you, analyse the situation at hand, and discuss techniques to help soothe your mind in a non-judgmental manner.

Most therapists have a tool kit comprising of whatever they have been trained in. Anyone seeing a counsellor or therapist should feel free to find out what training has been undertaken. No one should feel stuck with a counsellor or therapist, either. If you are not comfortable with their services after the first two to four sessions, it is okay to terminate and find someone else.

Personally, because of my mind battles, it made sense for me to embark on a Cognitive Behaviour Therapist Practitioner Certification (CBT), and in the process, Trauma and Advanced Behavioural Certifications.

CBT - Cognitive Behavioural Therapy

CBT is a form of talking therapy that aims to tackle thoughts, beliefs, feelings, and behaviour that may be negatively impacting a person's day to day activities and productivity. It arms you with various techniques for dealing and coping with presenting issues. CBT is a combination of how you think and what you do, and is popularly used to treat anxiety, depression, Obsessive Compulsive Disorder, Bipolar or Schizophrenia.

DBT - Dialectical Behaviour Therapy

Distress tolerance skills, emotional regulation, coping thoughts, mindfulness, interpersonal effectiveness, examining your core beliefs and self-limiting beliefs are all employed during this form of talk therapy.

Some of the skills mentioned above are a combination of CBT and DBT.

The Conscious and Subconscious Mind

The brain is one of God's unique, complex designs. It is divided into two distinct interconnected systems: the *conscious mind* and the *subconscious mind.*

The conscious mind is logical. Its actions are based on information received from the five senses: touch, feel, smell, sense, and taste. The conscious mind is responsible for thinking, analysis, and rationalisation. Think conscious mind, think logic. However, it DOES NOT control our actions.

The subconscious mind literally controls our actions exclusively. This part is primarily ruled by emotions and instinct, and its central role is to see that urges and needs, including reproduction, food, thirst, safety and intimacy, are met. A potent force, the subconscious doesn't reason or judge. It simply acts, often commanding your actions. The two can bring you success or failure, happiness or anxiety, achievement, or frustration.

Have you ever not asked someone on a date for fear of them saying no? Or not applied for a job because you feared failure? This is the subconscious mind at work. *You cannot outdo the image of yourself that is stored in the subconscious mind.* This is what often prevents us from succeeding. If we do not have a picture of our success in the unconscious mind, achieving consistent success is practically impossible.

You can use your conscious mind to shape your unconscious mind by overriding it. This is not an easy process. It requires consistency, but it can be done.

Let's examine a couple of scriptural examples.

Proverbs 23:7 *'For as he thinks in his heart, so is he. "Eat and drink!" he says to you, but his heart is not with you.'*

"Eat and drink!" he says to you [*Conscious mind]*
"But his heart is not with you" [*Subconscious mind]*

"Thinks" – the *Conscious mind* splits open, reasons out, calculates, reckons, and estimates.

His heart is the *subconscious mind* – his soul. It is his appetite, desire, emotion, and passion. It is this man's inner being.

Matthew 15:8 *'These people draw near to Me with their mouth and honour Me with* their *lips, but their heart is far from Me.'*

These people … honour Me with their lips - *Conscious*

But their heart is far from Me - *Subconscious*

Neuroplasticity

God's mercies are new every morning!

Did you know that your brain is constantly changing? The conscious and subconscious minds are carefully wired together so that old connections are continually breaking and new ones forming. In fact, one thing that determines how these connections form is your thoughts.

Neuroplasticity refers to structural and functional changes in the brain that happen due to new experiences. Because of its plasticity, also referred to as neuroplasticity, the brain can "rewire" and "re-organise" itself after brain damage as new connections are formed, terminating neural pathways to damaged areas.

The equivalent of this, from my perspective, is being renewed in the spirit of your mind. Another way of describing it, as we've said above, is 'putting on the new man' (Ephesians 4:23 and 24)

This further alludes to the fact that deep inside us is the ability to engage our minds to the point of emotional, mental, and psychological transformation. The way we think, rationalise, understand, and process information, can be overhauled, making it possible to defeat self-sabotaging thoughts and limiting self-beliefs, thereby winning our mental battles.

Emotional Regulation

Emotional regulation enables us to regulate anger, fear, sadness, frustration, depression, and other emotions, preventing negative thoughts from taking over our sense of reasoning, and feelings from driving negative or sometimes self-destroying behaviours. This has been a life saver that I practise regularly with myself and others who are closely related to me. Without it, one would keep flying off the handle and apologising for flaring up without applying any emotional brakes, even though the reason for the reaction may be right. With much practise and understanding, regulating my emotions within seconds is becoming much easier and being at peace is a common feature in my life.

Jesus' example in the garden of Gethsemane is to be commended, and there are many lessons from Matthew 26:36-38 (NIV):

> *"Then Jesus came with them to a place called Gethsemane, and told His disciples, 'Sit here while I go over there and pray.' And He took Peter and the two sons of Zebedee with Him, and he began to be grieved and distressed. Then He said to them, 'My soul is deeply grieved, to the point of death; remain here and keep watch with Me.'"*
>
> *"And being in anguish, he prayed more earnestly, and his sweat was like drops of blood falling to the ground."* Luke 22:44

Regardless of his emotional and somatic experiences, Jesus still went to the cross. He was able to regulate his emotions. What an example for you and me to follow!

Here are a few important tips to help you cope and adjust your reactions.

1. Name and recognise the emotion you are feeling.

2. Explore the hurt that emotion is creating or has created.

3. Intentionally increase your positive emotions by generating feel-good factors like positive affirmations and positive thinking.

4. Use coping thoughts to calm your mind.

5. Depending on the issue, you may need to confide in someone or talk some sense to yourself. (I highly recommend you practice this).

6. Remain mindful of your emotions and work them till you are at peace.

Reflections:

Are you willing to commit to doing the mind work?

Result

Reasons for saying you will/ won't

Take a moment to pause, get into a comfortable posture, relax, and meditate on your answers. Jot down steps you will take to improve your thought life. Remember your brain has the capacity to heal!!

---

[19] Genesis 2:17
[20] https://www.blueletterbible.org/lexicon/g4151/kjv/tr/0-1/
[21] John I9:30

Section Six

> *Winning the battle of your mind requires an anchor to stabilise and distract the mind until the desired change is achieved.*
>
> ***– Abbiih Oloyede***

Tips and Tools

Using STOP as an acronym, do the following:

- *S – Stop what you are thinking about immediately! Just pause for a moment.*

- *T – Take a Breath:* Notice your breathing as you breathe in and out.

- *O – Observe:* What thoughts are going through your mind right now?
  Where is your attention focused?
  What are you reacting to?
  What sensations do you notice in your body?

- *P – Pull Back: Put in Some Perspective*
  Look at the bigger picture
  What is another way of looking at this situation?

What would a trusted friend say to you right now?

Is this thought a fact or an opinion?

What is a more reasonable explanation?

How important is this?

How important will it be in six months?

Then practice this repeatedly.

Journaling

I always advocate capturing your thoughts in a journal. Journaling helps calm the mind and highlights blind spots. It is not unusual for emotional eureka! moments to occur during the writing and reflecting process.

Be Part of a Network

No one should walk alone. Find people you can talk to. A starting point could be joining a same interest group. Be intentionally friendly. The main point here is, don't stay isolated. Isolation doesn't help with mind matters.

Keep Moving

Don't let your experience control your waking moments. At some point, you must take the bull by the horns. Start by taking baby steps and, with persistence and consistency, you will slowly but surely win your mind battles.

Forgiveness is Vital

The action or process of forgiving or being forgiven is described by words including pardon, discharge, leniency, amnesty, mercy. Psychologists have long maintained that harbouring a grudge is not beneficial to emotional or physical health.

Forgiveness is **a complex emotion that does not always come naturally,** nor does it happen just because we tell someone we've forgiven them. It involves an internal change of heart. However, once we **learn** to forgive and **practice** forgiveness, we will find ourselves feeling free of heavy burdens and being more at ease.

Emotional and Cognitive Forgiveness

Emotional forgiveness has to do with being able to generate the feelings that will aid in letting go, while the cognitive aspect is all about logic and analysis.

> *'If you **forgive** the sins of any, they are forgiven them; if you retain the sins of any, they are retained.'* John 20:23

*'And **forgive** us our sins, for we also **forgive** everyone who is indebted to us....'* Luke 11:4

Steps to Forgiveness

- Recognise and acknowledge your emotions and feelings
- Consider how the hurt and pain has affected you. Don't rush this!!
- Accept that you cannot change the past. Don't sweep this under the carpet. There is no such thing as moving on.
- Determine whether you will forgive or not. Do you want to forgive? Be honest.
- Put yourself in the other person's shoes. (Quite challenging!)

- Note the lessons from this experience.
- Let it go. Keep a memorial in your heart or physical object, but let it go.

Epigenetics – Generational Curses

Epigenetics is **the study of how your behaviours and environment can affect the way your genes work**. Unlike genetic changes, epigenetic changes are reversible and do not alter your DNA sequence, but they can determine how your body reads a DNA sequence.

Today, the idea that a person's experience could alter their biology and their children and grandchildren's behaviours has gained serious traction. Hindrances and obstacles (generational curses) are mentioned in several places.

God warns that He is "...*a jealous God, punishing the children for the sin of the fathers to the third and fourth generation of those who hate me*[22]."

It sounds unfair for God to punish children for the sins of their fathers. However, there is more to it. The effects of sin are naturally passed down from one generation to the next, so, when a father has a sinful lifestyle, his children are likely to practice the same lifestyle. Implied in the warning of Exodus 20:5 is the fact that children will choose to repeat their fathers' sins.

The positive takeaway about epigenetics is that it is reversible. It should not be regarded as a death sentence but rather, with knowledge and support, look at steps you can take to completely reverse, manage, minimise, or delay the effect of any cross over of mental health challenges you may face because of your environment or upbringing.

Why don't Christians like Therapy?

Some Christians frown at the notion of therapy for varied reasons. From personal experience, the Word undoubtedly healed my mind before I made any self-diagnosis. Philippians 4:8 reframed my mind without support or intervention, but in essence, I used the verse for my cognitive rehearsal, such that whenever a thought showed up, recalling the verse terminated the negative thoughts.

There were so many 'aha!' moments during my Cognitive Behaviour Practitioner training as it became clear that most of the principles we discussed could be found in the Scriptures. The Psalms are full of what is known in CBT as coping thoughts, positive affirmations, and hope-filled words, to mention a few.

Prayer and meditation are recommended by most therapists, as there is emotional and mental strength in knowing you can talk and relate to a higher being. I touch the divine through constant prayer, reading my Bible, listening to Christian inspired music, sermons and asking for prayers from my Christian support network.

When asked, 'Why therapy?' my response is usually, 'Why do Christians divorce?' The fact that we are Christians should guarantee a happy marriage. However, this is not the case because of what I term as *relational dynamics* – the unique communication style adopted by a married couple or anyone in a close relationship with friends and family. Some refer to it as yin and yang. For any relationship to be successful, each party must be self-aware and conscious of how they come across.

For instance, it occurred to me to analyse my being quite impatient and irritable in my marriage. As mentioned earlier, marriage and close relationships display our biases, strengths, and weaknesses. Despite understanding my temperament and being self-aware, getting to the bottom of my nagging irritation became imperative. It was time to take the thought to the edge. No more repressing, sweeping away the thoughts, putting them on the shelf or writing about them in my journal to be dealt with later. It was time to deal with it, and deal with it, I did. By spending time querying, questioning, praying, reflecting, and meditating, it soon became apparent that being easily irritated was inherited from my mother. Today, emotional regulation helps me recalibrate quickly, faster, and more easily. I am still working on being less impulsive and impatient.

Reflections:

Which of the tools do you prefer?

Result

Take a moment to pause, get into a comfortable posture, relax, and meditate on your answers. Jot down steps you will take to improve your thought life. Remember your brain has the capacity to heal!!

[22] Exodus 20:5

Conclusion

As I reflect on the entire book, it is clear that the battle of the mind will forever be an issue with human beings. Past generations experienced mental and emotional turbulence, which resulted in the myriads of books, data, and articles on the mind. The present generation is experiencing the same turmoil on a more intense scale, and the advent of social media has added a twist with far-reaching consequences. Sadly, the unborn generation will likely deal with mind-related issues as well.

With the magnitude of this problem, I believe everyone should be armed with the basic information, tools, and suggestions to be able to act as a first responder to anyone in their vicinity who suffers from an emotional or mental crisis.

This book is a sneak preview of my personal journey. I use the tools and tips shared in it regularly. Sometimes, a simple one-minute emotional regulation will calm my mind. But more often, it takes continuous practice and utilisation of the skills to do so. It is not uncommon for my clients to tell me,

'Abbiih, I feel much better! You have been through this, and you know exactly what I am struggling with, so there is hope for me.'

My heart's desire is for every man, woman, boy or girl to know the importance and impact our thought life has on our emotions and behaviours. With the right knowledge, support, and the mind owner's determination, most of us can and **will** win the battle of the mind.

Bibliography

American Psychological Association. (n.d.). *Trauma*. Retrieved June 23, 2021, from APA: https://www.apa.org/topics/trauma

Bennett, A. a. (2022). *DIscover Your Temperament*. Retrieved June 28, 2022, from Temperament Quiz: https://www.temperamentquiz.com/

Cloud, H. (n.d.).

MIND. (2020, June). *Mental health facts and statistics*. Retrieved July 14, 2021, from https://www.mind.org.uk/information-support/types-of-mental-health-problems/statistics-and-facts-about-mental-health/how-common-are-mental-health-problems/#References

NHS. (n.d.). *Overview - Cognitive behavioural therapy (CBT)*. Retrieved June 30, 2021, from NHS.UK: https://www.nhs.uk/mental-health/talking-therapies-medicine-treatments/talking-therapies-and-counselling/cognitive-behavioural-therapy-cbt/overview/

NHS. (n.d.). *Overview - Obsessive compulsive disorder (OCD)*. Retrieved June 24, 2021, from NHS: https://www.nhs.uk/mental-health/conditions/obsessive-compulsive-disorder-ocd/overview/#overview)

NHS. (n.d.). *Treatment - Borderline personality disorder*. Retrieved June 30, 2021, from NHS UK: https://www.nhs.uk/mental-health/conditions/borderline-personality-disorder/treatment/

Psy.D., M. S. (2019, June 3). *What a Sticky Mind Means*. (J. Schrader, Editor) Retrieved June 28, 2022, from Psychology Today: https://www.psychologytoday.com/gb/blog/living-sticky-mind/201906/what-sticky-mind-means

What are intrusive thoughts? (n.d.). Retrieved June 23, 2021, from IESO digital health: https://www.iesohealth.com/en-gb/blog/what-are-intrusive-thoughts

Additional Scriptures for Meditation

"*The law of the Lord is perfect, converting the soul; The testimony of the Lord is sure, making wise the simple...*" Psalms 19:7

"*The troubles of my heart have enlarged; Bring me out of my distresses*!" Psalms 25:17

"*The Lord is my strength and my shield; My heart trusted in Him, and I am helped; Therefore, my heart greatly rejoices, And with my song I will praise Him*." Psalm 28:7

"*The Lord redeems the soul of His servants, And none of those who trust in Him shall be condemned.*" Psalm 34:22

"*And my soul shall be joyful in the Lord; It shall rejoice in His salvation.*" Psalm 35:9

Printed in Great Britain
by Amazon

30121502R00093